Libro para Colorear Aves para Adultos

Libro de colorear consciente del Birdwatcher

ADULT COLORING BOOKS

www.adultcoloringbooks.co

All rights reserved. No part of this document may be reproduced
Used or transmitted in any form or by any means, electronic or otherwise. This means you cannot photocopy any material ideas or tips that are provided in this book.

Adult Coloring Books
Published by Ciparum LLC

Libro para Colorear Aves para Adultos
Libro de colorear consciente del Birdwatcher
© 2016 Ciparum LLC
All rights reserved.
ISBN-10:1-63589-229-5
ISBN-13:978-1-63589-229-1

www.AdultColoringBooks.co

Other Books in this Series

Adult Coloring Books Series
Easter Bunny Secrets Adult Coloring Book
Mandala Coloring Book –Volume 1
Adult Coloring Book – Volume 2
Owls Coloring Book
Valentine's Day Secrets Adult Coloring Book
Mermaids Adult Coloring Book
Butterflies Adult Coloring Book

For more engaging activity books for Adults, visit:

www.adultcoloringbooks.co

www.ingramcontent.com/pod-product-compliance
Lightning Source LLC
Chambersburg PA
CBRC091204070526
44584CB00008B/333